MW01224137

VIKING ARCHAEOLOGY

DIGGING UP THE PAST

By : Shane Hultquist

First printing – October 2010

© 2010 – Shane Hultquist

ISBN : 978-0-9813230-0-8

This book is dedicated to my Mother, Father and Grandparents, who without their financial support, this journey would not have been possible. It is also dedicated to my close friends who heard me tell my story over and over and at least never told me they got sick of hearing it or seeing the photos.

I would also like to thank my professor in Sweden, Dan Carlsson as well as the other students that took this course. It was a fabulous journey, and I am glad we got to do it together.

TABLE OF CONTENTS

Introduction

In the summer of 2007, I had the privilege to attend a 3 week Viking archaeology course on the island of Gotland in Sweden. Having been interested in Viking history for many years, but having no formal training in archaeology, I was a bit daunted by this task. The course was designed for those that were beginners straight through to grad students working on a masters in archaeology.

When I had originally planned on taking this trip, I knew that my ancestry had roots in Sweden, but did not know any details. After announcing my plans to my family, my father found a birth certificate of my great-grandfather from a small town named Växjö. Just prior to arriving in Stockholm for my ferry ride to Visby, I spent a night in Växjö. I had hoped to visit the library or the ancestry centre that they have, but unfortunately they were all closed by the time I arrived, and my train left early the next day, so I could not get the opportunity to investigate any further. I did however find my last name in the phone book. If it had not been too late, and if I had more time, I would have contacted what could be distant relatives. But alas, it was not meant to be.

I will return to Sweden someday soon, and I hope to bring my father and grandfather to Sweden so they can visit our homeland and experience it the way I did.[1]

What follows now is an account of my experiences and finds during my 3 weeks of being an archaeology student in Sweden.

---

[1] At the time of publishing, my Grandfather had passed away, so this was no longer an option.

Chapter 1 – The Arrival

The start of my journey did not begin in Sweden, but in Denmark. Being it is not entirely relevant to the archaeology course, I will only briefly describe some of the events that took place there.

I arrived by plane into Copenhagen, Denmark after a gruelling 8 hour flight. However, there was a 6 hour time difference for me to contend with as well. I spent an early night in my hotel room before embarking on a brief journey around Denmark.

On my first day in Denmark, I visited the Viking Ship Museum in Roskilde, Denmark. This was an experience that I wanted to have while overseas. I toured all the museum areas and went on a guided tour which was nice. Afterwards I went to the dock area and took a trip on a Viking ship (Figure 1). We were all given life jackets for safety. We did have to row the

Figure 1 – Viking Ship in Roskilde

ship out to the open fjord and then they put up our sail. It was hard work, but well worth it.

After a few days in Denmark, it was time for me to depart to Sweden. I hopped on the RailEurope train which would be taking me to Växjö. After my stay there overnight, I would continue on to Stockholm. Total train ride was about 6 hours. I was not staying long in Stockholm as I had to catch the ferry to Gotland later that evening. I arrived at the ferry and found that there were some issues with my pre-purchased ticket. The dates were a bit off from what I had calculated. They adjusted my ticket with no issues and I was off to Gotland. Upon arrival, I was to meet some of the others that were on the course with me.

Allow me to backtrack for a moment. Regarding my fellow students on this course, we were communicating via email with each other and I found that another of the students was from Ottawa. We had decided to get together before leaving a few times to chat and have a few beers together. It was great to have someone over there that I already knew.

So when I arrived by ferry to Visby, I was greeted by a fellow student and also one of the instructors. I picked up my luggage and we were off to the Visby airport to get another student before heading to our cabins.

Many other students were already settled in their cabins. These cabins were pre-assigned for us. I had hoped that my roommate would be the other Ottawa student, but it was not. Instead I met someone new which was nice too. Most cabins had 3 to a cabin, but we were the odd cabin out, so we only had the 2 of us. That gave us only slightly more room to maneuver around our tiny cabin.

Figure 2 – Baltic Sea from Slite

The first thing I noticed about our "home" for the next few weeks was the view (figure 2). Our cabins were located almost directly on the Baltic Sea. There was a small dock that led right out into the water, and a beautiful rocky shoreline just outside our doors. This made for some very cool evenings as the breezes coming in off the sea were not overly enjoyable.

Our first night on the island was mostly sitting around, getting to know each other, sharing a few pints of beer and then getting ourselves ready for bed. The beds were quite small, even for someone as short as I am. A few of the others that were considerably taller than I was must have had a hard time sleeping.

We woke up in the morning and headed off to explore the small town of Slite where we were staying. It was Sunday and we knew that class would be starting tomorrow. The sky was a bit overcast, but that did not break down spirits at all. We also had our transportation delivered to us so we could get to our dig site in the morning. We all had old style bicycles.

Now, I had not ridden a bicycle in quite some time, but it's like the old saying goes, so I decided to give it a shot. The distance to our dig site was only about 3 KM, but there were some stretches along a highway and also some really nasty hills. I was pretty sore after riding to the site. This will lead us directly into Day 1 of the dig.

Chapter 2 – The Site

Upon arrival at the site, the first thing we noticed was a trailer set up in a small courtyard outside of a beautiful house. This trailer was our field office for the duration of the dig. Our first day was a basic orientation of the site, and procedures on what we would be doing over the next 3 weeks.

Our professor had a slideshow and video to show us of archaeology work from previous excavations that he performed on Gotland over the years. He also gave us a detailed history of the area that we were going to be working on.

In this particular area, Klints Farm in the Othem parish in Gotland, we were excavating what was thought to be an old Viking age farmhouse. The original farmhouse is shown below from a painting inside the restored house (figure 3).

Figure 3 – Original Klints Farm

We were given a tour of the farmhouse and a brief history of the Klints farm area. The land we were going to be excavating backs onto what is now Slite Golfklubb. Our actual dig site was situated just off the green from one of the holes. We had to be very careful as we moved out from under our tent cover so we would not get hit by golf balls.

After our tour of the farmhouse, we were taken to the excavation site. There we met with Tove Eriksson (Assistant Project Archaeologist) and Field Archaeologist Anna Pettersson. There was an existing team already doing some excavations on part of the site and we got to watch them briefly and were shown the type of artifacts that they had already uncovered.

Figure 4 – Excavation Site

Our primary focus on this site was to discover how this building was built, what type of building it was, and of course to catalog all artifacts that we find along the way. Every small object found helps to determine the type of structure we were dealing with. This included small animal bones (likely chicken or some other small animal) and other forms of "garbage" they would have left behind or buried.

Figure 4 shows an image of the excavation site with the tent covering it. The group in the foreground of the picture was the existing archaeology team and in the back, under the tented area was our team. The large pile of earth in the top right of the photo is the top layer of dirt/grass removed from the site prior to our arrival.

On our first day there we were put to work right away. We were given small trowels and plastic buckets to gently remove areas of dirt to later be sifted (figure 5).

Figure 5 – Sifting for artifacts

The process of sifting through the soil is long and arduous. You start by taking the bucket of dirt that you removed from the site, dump this into a sifting mechanism (small metal grate similar to a screen door) and rolling the sifter back and forth letting all the loose dirt fall into a pile under the sifter. You continue to do this and examine the material remaining in the sifter. The person that is third from the right in this photo is doing just that.

Some items are discarded right away (small rocks, twigs, roots and such) and sometimes it can be quite difficult to figure out if something is a rock, twig or bone. After a few days of doing this however, it became more apparent.

After a long first day of digging and sifting, nobody in our group found anything of importance. We all climbed on our bikes, hot, sweaty and dirty and rode back to our cabins. The bike ride took us about half an hour. We showered, changed into some new clothes and all went out for dinner at a local restaurant in Slite. We recounted our first day on the dig site and most of us commented that we were quite sore after doing all the biking and the kneeling down while digging.

We decided to do some grocery shopping so we could bring nice lunches with us to the site over the next week. I dreaded riding this bike every day, so I inquired about the discounted car rental that we could get from being students. Tuesday I would have to ride my bike back to the dig site, so I just had to deal with that, but a car would be forthcoming.

Chapter 3 – The finds

We now fast forward to day 3 of our dig. Day 2 was mostly instructional as it was raining most of the day. We chose to stay indoors and learn a bit more history and also learn how to log finds once we actually find something worth logging. It was a good thing we did this as day 3 was a somewhat prosperous day for finds.

Shortly after our morning coffee break (and in Sweden they are apparently very serious about their coffee breaks) we were back digging and sifting and more

Figure 6 – English Silver Coin (front)

digging and more sifting. You get the idea. After about an hour of this, I saw something metallic looking in my sifter. I stopped sifting immediately and brushed some dirt off of what I was sure was going to be a great find.

From our group, I was the first to actually find a coin (figures 6 and 7). It was in pretty good shape considering it was almost 1,000 years old.

After finding the coin, our professor decided to sit us down for a bit and give us a bit of a history on this particular coin. The coin was minted between 978 and 1016 C.E. It bears the name "Edelred" on it, which translates to Æthelred II. Æthelred II was also known as Æthelred the Unready. The story behind this is as follows.

Figure 7 – English Silver Coin (back)

King Æthelred was King of England from 978-1013 and the nickname "Unready" comes from the Anglo-Saxon unread meaning "ill-advised". A band of Viking warriors set to raid the English and when they approached King Æthelred offered to pay them "Danegeld" or "Danish Tax". Danegeld was a tribute paid to Viking raiders to stop them from actually raiding. As the story goes, they were given a large sum of Danegeld to leave. They honorably did so and took the coins back with them. However, the next year they decided to raid once again. When they approached, Æthelred offered to pay them once again to leave. Seeing as how they were getting money, they chose to take the silver and leave. They continued to do this over and over until Æthelred had used up quite a bit of the silver that England had. Finally he had had enough and ordered a massacre of Danish settlers in 1002. The raids stopped after this, and in 1013, Æthelred fled to Normandy and was replaced by Sweyn, who was also the King of Denmark. Æthelred returned a year later after the death of Sweyn.

How all the silver ended up in Gotland was another interesting tale. Gotland is situated in the middle of the Baltic Sea between Sweden (to the West) and Finland (to the North-East), Russia (to the East), Poland (to the South), and Germany (to the South West). Gotland was a definite trading site for travelers coming up from Byzantium and Istanbul. It would make sense that the West (England, Ireland, Norway, Denmark and others) would have traded silver for goods coming from the East.

A few years prior to our excavation course, our professor was involved with the largest silver horde find in Gotland. It was at the Spillings farm and the total silver horde weighed in at over 67 kilograms (148 pounds).

The Spillings horde is thought to have been money that was stolen during a time when taxes were being collected. The robbers took the silver, likely killing those that were collecting it, and hid it under or just outside a house. These people would have likely gone on a long trade somewhere and never made it back, leaving the silver buried until 2005.

One interesting point is that many of the coins found are in or near farmhouses ranging from 700-1100 C.E.

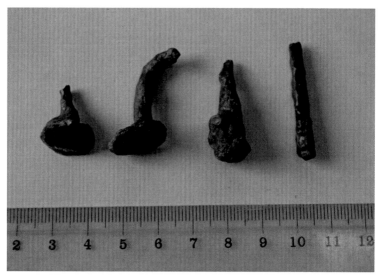

Figure 8 – Rivets and Nails from Viking Age

Most of this land has been ploughed and worked for over 100 years, yet these items still remain. There are still reports of people working in their garden and unearthing a silver coin from Viking age. When this happens, generally an archeological team is called in to excavate the site to determine more how this island looked over 1,000 years ago.

Figure 8 shows some rivets and nails that were found on our dig site as well. These were made of iron and for being over 1,000 years old, have been quite well preserved.

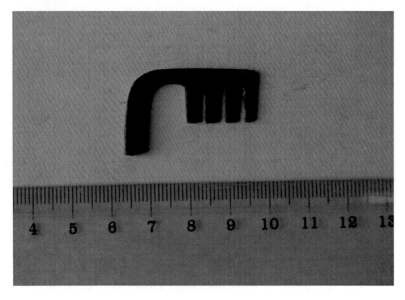

Figure 9 - Iron Key

An iron key was found on our 4th or 5th day that was very well preserved. Keys such as this would have been kept by the wife. In Viking society, women were the holders of the "keys" to the homestead. The reasons for this were that the men would regularly go out raiding or trading and may never return.

Figure 10 depicts a very well preserved axe head. While it is not very large, it was probably a small tool for either making other tools, or for very delicate work.

Figure 10 - Iron Axe Head

As the days progressed, more and more artifacts were found on our dig site. On the 5th day of digging, we started to find formations of large rocks that appeared to be holding something up. This was determined to be post holes for the dwelling. The professor started mapping these out to try and determine the shape and size of the dwelling we were working on. More and more postholes were coming up as the days went on.

Figure 11 - Post Holes

(figure 11 depicts where two posts would have been held up by the rocks)

One of the great finds we had on the 5th day was when one of our groups discovered something small, but solid. As they excavated it closer and closer, it turned out to be a furnace of some sort. It was where metals would have been melted down to make other objects. Figure 12 shows the furnace shortly after excavating the top of it. It does not look too impressive in this picture, but we took this and extrapolated what it would have looked like if it were intact.

After finding the furnace we started to find more and more treasures in the dig. We found many more coins from the King Ethelred II era, as well as several Persian coins. These would have been acquired in various trades along the Viking trade routes of the time.

Other items that were found included nails and rivets, several more keys, a few belt decorations, a sewing needle (quite large actually), what appeared to me to be a spear head, but could have easily been a regularly used tool, and some animal bone pieces.

One piece that was found was a small piece of a bone comb with many of the tines still intact. It was only a few inches long, but it was easily seen to be a comb. On our way back to the field office to catalog the finds for the day, the person carrying it had tripped over a root and we lost the comb fragment. We looked for about an hour in the tall grass, but it was to be lost until someone else may discover it in a few years.

Figure 12 - Furnace

Chapter 4 – Disaster Strikes

On our first weekend off, we spent some time travelling around and the Sunday staying indoors quite a bit for our first Gotlandic storm. We were not quite sure what to expect being on an island in the middle of the Baltic Sea, but we prepared for lots of rain. We were not disappointed in the amount of rain that we got.

We headed to the dig site, still raining a bit, but very lightly. We were quite wet when we arrived and all huddled into the field office to have some coffee and stay warm. Our Professor told us that there were issues down at the site that we had to take care of. Apparently the storm caused some havoc with our tent.

We walked down to the site (figure 13). The first thing we noticed was that the tent that we were using for shelter was missing. It had blown over in the storm. Now it was time to go find our tent.

It had blown about 30-40 feet away from the actual dig site and some of the poles were pretty twisted up. After looking at the dig site, we realized that something major had happened in the area. We were then told by our Leaders that a tornado had come through the area and after re-examining the ground, that was pretty evident. (figure 14)

The tornado had destroyed several of the posthole locations by dragging the heavy poles from the large tent through the rock formations. Fortunately all of these were already mapped out and drawn so that the actual information was not lost.

We spent the next hour or so reassembling the tent so that we would not be assaulted by golf balls while we continued to work. The hard part was sifting through the wet dirt this day. It was not much fun, and we were all a little depressed this day. But, like any good team, we persevered and continued to work. We spent our afternoon in the office for a lecture so at least we were able to stay dry.

Figure 13 - After the Storm

Figure 14 – The Damage is done

Chapter 5 – It's all fun and games until...

Well, nobody lost their eye or anything, but one of our dig-mates did get a nasty allergic reaction to something which made her have to put an eye-patch on for a bit. But that's the worst that happened, so it's all good.

As for the fun and games, that came on the next weekend. We happened to be in Gotland for the World Championships of Kubb. This is a game I had researched a while before travelling to Sweden and had lots of fun playing it. This has nothing to do with archaeology directly, but it does have some significance, so it goes in this book.

Kubb is a game that is played in many backyards on Gotland, as well as other parts of Sweden. It's similar to playing horseshoes, lawn darts, lawn bowling and the like. These are the basics of the game.

The field is 8 meters by 5 meters. There is a king piece set up in the centre of the field. Each short side of the field has 5 "kubb" pieces set up. These are all about 4 inches tall. Each team then takes turns throwing batons or sticks at the kubb pieces on the other side. If they knock down a piece, after their turn is over, the other team throws the kubb pieces back to the other side of the field where they are up righted. They then throw the batons trying to knock down the "field kubb" pieces first. When one team has knocked over all the kubb pieces on the other side, they then try to knock down the king piece, thus winning the game.

We decided to enter a team in the World Championships and called our team ArkeoKubb (Our course was being presented by ArkeoDok, so we found this to be appropriate). The unfortunate part was the tournament starting on the Friday, so we had to convince our professor to give us a day off so we could play in the tournament. This turned out to be easier than we thought as he had a team entered in the tournament as well.

We travelled down to the South end of the island in a few hours and saw the setup of the tournament. It was pretty impressive with over 50 fields set up and 4 teams at each field. It was a round robin tournament at each field with the ultimate victors there moving on.

I don't mind saying at this point that we were not very good in the tournament. Partially because we were inexperienced, partially because we had been given some Gotlandsdricka prior to playing (this is a Gotlandic version of homemade beer) and partially because it was raining a bit, just enough to make the fields wet.

We did however win one game out of 3, but that was not enough to advance to the next round. We ended up staying for a little bit, watched a few games and then went on our way to do a bit of exploring on the island. After all, we had a day off.

One last note on the Kubb World Championships, we did get awarded the Judges Fair Play award for that day. It was an honor just to play, and getting the award was just a nice bonus.

We had several maps of points of interest on the island, as well as some great tips from our Professor. Our first stop was a gravesite that contained several cairns. The following is taken from the plaque at the base of one of the cairns.

"Uggarde Rojr is the largest cairn in Gotland and one of the largest anywhere in Sweden. Gotland has more than 1 300 cairns, of which about 400 are classes as 'Great Cairns'. Most of them are now to be seen along what at the time were the coast and shipping lines. Uggarde Rojr is 7 metres high and 50 metres in diameter. To the southwest are several large boulders which may once have been standing stones. Close to the cairn are also smaller graves, known as stone settings.

When constructed these cairns were about 250 metres from the shoreline. In that position they must have been excellent navigation marks, and this cairn commands an extensive view over the heathland and out to sea."

(figure 15) shows the Uggarde Rojr cairn with one of my fellow students standing beside it. It helps to show the size of this particular cairn.

From what we learned, many of the cairns have been excavated already and the artifacts cataloged and stored at one of the various museums. However, there was no more information regarding these cairns about who or what was stored inside them.

Figure 15 – Uggarde Rojr – largest cairn in Gotland

The next stop on our tour involved a small Viking village named "Stavgard". The following is an excerpt from their website.

The spring of 1975 a group of secondary school students found a silver treasure from 900 A.D., on a pasture nearby the bay of Bandelunda in Burs pastoral. According to the legend a powerful Viking chief "Stavar the Great" were to have lived here on this place called Stavgard. During the Viking era Stavgard had a large harbor. Excavations from the 1950's and 80's show evidence of intense trade in this well hidden harbor. Many silver artifacts, house foundations, boat rivets, and a "shell house," which functioned as boat house for Viking ships, have been found. The area still remains largely unexcavated.

1976 the non-profit organization of Stavgard was founded. Since the beginning of the 80's the organization runs a spring and fall camp together with the Gotland Board of Education. The organization strives to promote an understanding of prehistoric crafts and techniques, and to further the development of historic camps on Gotland and the Swedish mainland. During the years since its founding, the organization has built a complete Iron-age village. The houses are reconstructions from various periods of the Iron-age.

This was an experience that I enjoyed immensely and has made me want to pursue creating a small village like this in Canada to honor Leif Eriksson who landed in what is now Newfoundland in or around the year 1003 c.e.

The reconstructed houses were beautifully done, and I could have seen staying here overnight to enjoy what life would have been like for the Vikings.

Figure 16 – Iron Age House

Figure 16 shows one of the Iron Age houses at Stavgard. The base of the dwelling was made of relatively flat rocks to build a base, gradually leading to very flat rocks to build the walls. A wooden frame was then put in place for a door as well as a roof. On the roof, grass and sod was put down to aid in insulation as well as to keep rain out. The rain would likely soak up into the sod and the grass would grow right on the roof of the house. The top of the roof was open on both ends to allow smoke from the fires that were in the centre of the house to keep them warm and to cook on.

Stavgard had several houses of different construction types. Some were made almost entirely from wood, whereas others were made from multiple combinations. Some were single room dwellings, whereas others had a separate kitchen from the sleeping/eating quarters.

Within the Viking village, there was a building dedicated to making yarn from raw sheep wool, one building as a dedicated smithy for making metal tools and other utensils, and one outbuilding as a kitchen and craft area. Previous children that stayed at Stavgard have carved and painted runes in various places as part of their education at Stavgard.

There is a small area that was dedicated to the artwork of the previous students which included both picture

Figure 17 – Carvings and statues at Stavgard

and rune stones, statues of various Norse Gods and Godesses as well as shields and other items (figure 17).

Our journey continued after this to a gravesite that was clearly marked on our map, but was not clearly visible as we drove past it. We came back and explored the area as best we could.

Many of the graves in this area were marked with stones arranged in the shape of a longship. This is reminiscent of Viking burials where people of high standing were buried in a ship with all of the possessions they would need in the afterlife or they were put on a functioning ship with those possessions

Figure 18 – Viking Burial Site

and burned at sea. Figure 18 shows an image of the burial site. A photograph can not do the structure much justice.

At this burial site, there was also another cairn. Not quite as impressive as the Uggarde Rojr cairn, but this was somewhat unique in that the cairn was surrounded by large stones in a complete circle (figure 19).

Figure 19 – Ringed Cairn

This ended our long journey on our own, but we were to be treated by our professor to a full day excursion of the island narrated by all of our instructors.

Chapter 6 – The Excursion

Our first stop on our excursion of Gotland sites was Trullhalsar. Trullhalsar is a burial ground of about 340 small cairns from the 7th century CE. When it was in use it was located by the seashore, but now it is in the middle of an enchanting wood.

The cairns at Trullhalsar are somewhat unique in their construction (figure 20) These cairns are round, but they have walls built with very flat stones and then larger rocks piled on top of the entire structure. These cairns have almost all been excavated, or raided by looters at one point or another, but they were always rebuilt in the same style that they were originally found.

Figure 20 – Cairn at Trullhalsar

Several other graves at Trullhalsar were of similar fashion as the gravesite we visited on the previous day. They had stones raised in the shapes of longships. Some of the graves are marked simply with large stones at what appear to be cardinal compass points (North, South, East and West). One oddity that was found there was a line of stones that there were no graves for, but all the stones were placed in a perfect line. The assumption of this was they were stones waiting to be used to mark other graves, but were never used (figure 21).

Figure 21 – Stones placed at Trullhalsar

Our next stop on the excursion was an old 13th century church. The following information is taken from a historical plaque at the front of the church.

Anga Church is a uniformly Romanesque structure from the early 13th century. The proportions of the nave are conspicuous – it is scarcely the length of the chancel and is shorter than the tower. This is explained by the fact that the nave extends all the way to the west end and the tower is raised above the western part.

The church has one of the best preserved medieval interiors on Gotland. The mural paintings date from the late 13th and mid 15th centuries. Notable among the furnishings are the late 14th century reredos, the 15th century rood, and the 13th century limestone font. The pulpit was made in the late 17th century, and the pews in the 18th century.

One item that I noticed when I first walked into this church, besides the small size of the interior, was the rune carvings on the walls. There was an entire script along the wall facing the doorway. The other item that interested me was the grave marker at the front of the church. It was a tomb cover (figure 22) and was carved with runes as well.

Figure 22 – Tomb Cover with Runes

Figure 23 – Pulpit at Anga Church

Our next stop was at Torsburgen which is a large hill-fort in the Kräklingbo parish. The fort is approximately 1.2 square kilometers which is the Nordic region's largest hill-fort. It is surrounded on the west, north and east side by an almost 30 meter high cliff. On the southern side, there is a 4-7 meter high and 2 kilometer long wall made of limestone. There were several "gates" leading into the centre of the fort.

Excavations of the inner area of this fort did not reveal anything. In areas where it appeared there may have been structures, nothing was found. Excavations carried out on the cold wall found residues that were carbon dated to the period surrounding the birth of Christ.

It is believed that this structure was used to protect a castle up until the Viking age.

After walking along the limestone wall for a while, we were taken to the Northern side of the cliff. We climbed up the side (almost 30 meters high) and were treated with a spectacular view of Gotland (figure 24)

Figure 24 – View of gotland from Torsburgen Northern cliff

The next site we visited on our tour was the next site that our professor was looking at excavating. The only remains of the house that are still above ground were a stone fireplace and the post holes where the beams would have been. We did some measurements and drew the outline map of the house while we were there.

The house that we were working with would have been last used around 750 years ago. Initial excavations of the area found fishnet weights, horseshoes, coins and glass.

At this site there was a well that was found by archaeologists that was dated back to the middle ages. When they poked around in the well they found several coins. These coins were dated from the 1970s. That is not a typo; these were recent coins in there. They figured that people may have used this as a modern-day wishing well.

The water in the well was crystal clear and we all were told we could have a drink from this well. We did, and the water was quite cold and very clear.

Our next stop was at the last standing picture stones on Gotland. These stones have not been removed and brought to the museum, but left as a marker for where they originally stood.

The main stone stands over 3.7 meters high. When we were up close to it, we could still see the carvings on the stone. This type of stone would have been painted as well, with very intricate drawings. These particular stones were dated to the 11th century.

The last site we visited on our excursion was a recreation of several Viking age houses. The first was a typical longhouse, made with wood, stones and sod.

Figure 25 – standing picture stones

Figure 26 – Recreation of a Viking Longhouse

The door frame of this house stood just less than 6 feet high. The top part of this house that can be seen in figure 26 is the ventilation for the fire pit inside the structure.

Inside of the longhouse is a very long picnic table that extends along the majority of the house itself (figure 27).

The next house that was recreated was made almost entirely of straw and wood. As can be seen in figure 28, the house is an "A" frame style house and was not very large inside.

Figure 27 – Inside the longhouse

Figure 28 – "A" frame style Viking age house

Figure 29 – Inside the "A" frame house

Chapter 7 – Our big find

In the third week of the excavation of Klints Farm, we finally found what we had been hoping for. We didn't find a huge treasure of silver coins like the Spillings horde, nor did we find any bodies buried on our site. What we did find however was one of the original posts from the building.

We weren't sure at first that this was a post. However, the evidence before us was pretty clear. There was a piece of wood in one of the postholes. The wood was very well preserved, and we had to take care as we excavated around this post. We were able to dig pretty deep and remove the wood from the posthole.

We did find out later that the wood was indeed carbon dated to around 1150 c.e.

This was exciting as we now had confirmation of the postholes and were able to construct a diagram of the building that was here. It turned out to be a very small building, and was likely and out-building from a main house.

Chapter 8 – The dig is over...for now

The dig in my estimation was a great success. I didn't find any graves, but I did find some coins, and we did find what it was we were looking for. On my last weekend in Gotland we took a trip to Visby to enjoy the medieval week festivities.

When we arrived in Visby, it was like we took a trip back in time. Among the most notable historical remains are the 3.4 km long stone wall called *Ringmuren* ("the Ring Wall") that encircles the city and the old church ruins.

The name "Visby" comes from the Old Norse Vis, (genitive singular of Vi) meaning sacrificial place, and by, meaning "city".

The earliest history of Visby is uncertain, but it is known to have been a centre of merchandise around 900 AD. It was inhabited as early as the stone age, probably because of the access to fresh water and a natural harbour.

In the 12th century, Visby Cathedral, dedicated to Saint Mary, was constructed. It was reshaped in the 13th century to its current appearance, and was officially opened in 1225 by the bishop of the Swedish city of Linköping. Several other churches were also constructed in the ensuing centuries. The city flourished, thanks to the German Hanseatic League.

The work on the ring wall was likely begun in the 12th century. Around 1300 it was rebuilt to reach its current height, acquiring the characteristic towers, although some towers were not constructed until the 15th century. The ringwall is still largely intact.

In 1361, Gotland was conquered by Valdemar IV of Denmark and Visby became a Danish city. Important as it was, some setbacks occurred. In 1391, 1394 and 1398 it was taken and plundered by the Victual Brothers, pirates who sailed the Baltic Sea. In 1411, King Eric of Pomerania had the castle of Visborg constructed, and settled himself there for twelve years, during which the city virtually became a pirates nest, and the commerce halted. As of 1470, the Hanseatic League rescinded Visby's status as a Hanseatic town.

In 1525, the final blow came. The merchants of Visby were in a feud with Lübeck in what is now Germany. The Lübeckers burned down all Visby's churches except the cathedral. The ruins have been preserved until this day, adding their gravity to the modern city.

Gotland was again conquered by Sweden in 1645 at the Treaty of Brömsebro, after 300 years of Danish rule. The city developed slowly as things were left as they were. In the mid 18th century some attempts were made by Swedish government officials to improve living standards, but little was accomplished. Not until the early 19th century did Visby once again attract commerce and a harbour industry. At the same time - 1808 - Gotland was conquered by Russia, but was peacefully taken back by the Swedes after only a couple of months.

The previous passage was courtesy of Wikipedia.org

Figure 30 – Ruins of a church in Visby

Figure 31 – Outside of another ruined church in Visby

Figure 32 – Stocks and Nithing pole outside a restaurant

Figure 32 depicts a nithing pole. A nithing pole was used to curse ones enemies. It traditionally has a horse head on top of the pole and the skin of the horse wrapped around the pole. The horse head would be faced towards the enemies.

Egils saga depicts the use of a nithing pole as shown below.

"And when all was ready for sailing, Egil went up into the island. He took in his hand a hazel-pole, and went to a rocky eminence that looked inward to the mainland. Then he took a horse's head and fixed it on the pole. After that, in solemn form of curse, he thus spake: 'Here set I up a curse-pole, and this curse I turn on king Eric and queen Gunnhilda. (Here he turned the horse's head landwards.) This curse I turn also on the guardian-spirits who dwell in this land, that they may all wander astray, nor reach or find their home till they have driven out of the land king Eric and Gunnhilda.' This spoken, he planted the pole down in a rift of the rock, and let it stand there. The horse's head he turned inwards to the mainland; but on the pole he cut runes, expressing the whole form of curse." - Egils Saga, Chapter LXXV

Figure 33 – Inside of a turret wall in Visby

Figure 34 – Inside the medieval restaurant in Visby

ISBN 978-0-9813230-0-8

Manufactured by Amazon.ca
Acheson, AB

14960897R00036